Conducting Out-Of-Box Market Research Studies

How data science & predictive analysis helps organization in new age

FARID PREMANI

ABOUT THE AUTHOR

Farid Premani takes us through a myriad of information on how and why new age companies should use data science predictive analysis. Each page beholds a well of information that helps market research companies benefit in their project endeavours in more ways than one innovatively using modern research tools and analysis through big data'

'Farid Premani, as an expert consultant on market research, uses this book as an outlet to share all his expertise and professionalism to create this bible for agencies and independent research consultants. He has given us a detailed flow of structure to make it easier for even the common businesses and start-up agencies to learn and implement expertise of data research and understanding what customer wants in 2016'

CONTACT AUTHOR

You can contact Farid Premani

By addressing mail at

ALEEDEX RESEARCH & CONSULTING GROUP

9800 Centre Parkway suite 625 Houston, TX USA

Email: farid@aleedex.com

CONTENTS

CHAPTER 1

STRATEGIC APPROACH TO MARKETING RESEARCH

Most business enterprise *leaders and* entrepreneurs will not *do a* ample job using the industry analysis component of their *strategic* planning. You can find a number of motives at the rear of *this:*

1*)* It truly is *not* actual interesting *(*until you're the *analytical, data-head* kind*)*

2*)* It might be amazingly high-priced *(and* we would like to save *the* spending plan for the entertaining things*)*

3*)* We're scared of *what* we would obtain *out (*it may be simpler to build *a* see on the marketplace we want *than to* experience the reality of your industry *realities).*

And, for those *of you who do* go through *the* significant effort *of* industry investigation, *scouring the* stories *from Jupiter, Gartner, or other* marketplace *watchdogs,* you're still lacking *the boat. This* world-wide examine the marketplace is essential, but not complete.

Except you've got unlimited *budgets (and* we would love to speak with *you* in case you *do), the* crucial move *of* current market study cannot *be short-changed.* To help make certain you've lined the many *bases,* consider *these* four procedures for the comprehensive, *holistic* marketplace exploration energy*:*

one. Survey Customers *and* probable customers, in addition to *colleagues in or* around *your* industry *or* target industry. Among the best market place investigation resources you may have, *is* your very own consumer base *and sphere of* impact. Conduct a web study *(of* no more than five questions*)* targeted at *pulling* potential traits *from this* worthwhile source. Request *them,* among *other* factors *a)* what the most crucial aspect *is* for purchasing a product *like yours; b)* exactly what is the largest *hurdle* they'll experience *in* upcoming *12-months; and/or c)* should they *could* change *your* goods and services, *what would they* like to *see (and why).* Pick 3 from the most critical study inquiries and also have *your* revenue team simply call individuals shoppers *who* did not answer to the net study to find the answers.

2. Obtain Workforce Input It is vital to include *your* inner staff

when conducting a industry research undertaking. Whether it's customer service who will go within the *"feet-on-the street"* developments *they* hear each day, *your* merchandise team that are *immersed* from the rising trends for his or her solution, *or your* government *or* sales team *who* normally *"hob nob"* while using the people today *who know,* you can come across critical data points that should *be* considered in your advertising approach. It is actually crucial *to solicit this* feed-back Independently instead of *as* group enter. We find *that when* requested for a group *you* either provide the quiet individuals *not feeding* into the method, or else you *have* these types of *a* general response *as* not to *be* appropriate. When you've collected the entire person suggestions, *compile* the outcomes *into* just one document *and* overview *for completeness,* regularity, *and consensus.* Wherever *consensus is* missing, address as a *team-using* the data from the *other* analysis ways to guide the way in which.

3. Examine *The* Levels of competition *(*take into consideration *"secret shopping"* to obtain the *"real experience").* We're normally told *by our* customers *"we know our* competition.*" Then, as our* advertising crew scientific tests *and "secret shops" the* levels of competition on their *behalf,* a completely different photo *unveils* by itself. It is important *to* a successful advertising and marketing system *that we not make assumptions about our* competitors *(who* they are really, *how they* place by themselves, *their strengths/weaknesses,* etcetera.*).* If you don't possess the assets *to* perform a thorough aggressive examine, hire someone that *can. We* assure it can *be enlightening,* as well as worthwhile on the investigate you will need on your advertising strategy.

4. Examine The industry *(*focus *on* facts *that* implies measurement, developments, and wish*).* It truly is this process where by *most* marketers emphasis *all* in their notice. *And,* while we do not feel *it* alone presents a whole enough image, *we do* recognize it is vital in your *strategic* planning. *When* assessing the marketplace point of view, start off *with trade associations, publications, and* exploration businesses targeted on the market.

Lots of you can not afford to pay for *the* experiences *or* costs with the investigation businesses covering *your* sector, *but* never *be discouraged.* Almost all of *the* stories *have* no cost govt *summaries* that will *get you* what you need. Once you *have* collected, *compiled, and analyzed* the knowledge *from all* four of such study techniques, you can choose to *then summarize* the significant details within the investigate segment within your Marketing and advertising Strategy. *This holistic* method of market place analysis provides you with almost everything you may need to make *an* efficient *and* efficient marketing *roadmap!*

Go-To-Market Approaches is often a useful resource heart *for* income *and* advertising and marketing professionals *and* company *leaders. Our* tools, *templates, and* products and services assist companies obtain massive *aspirations with* constrained *budgets.*

CHAPTER 2

HOW TO DECIDE RIGHT MODE FOR YOUR RESEARCH STUDY

How often with your enterprise crew meetings targeted at improving advancement *and earnings,* have you listened to somebody suggest performing *a* market study analyze*?* Often a specific type of study *of some* form is recommended, perhaps *a conjoint* or even a *segmentation,* or maybe a pleasure study. *The scope* of the analyze could be consistent with the particular region of debate, maybe solution *oriented, or positioning and communications* associated, or perhaps path to market place difficulties, *but* progressively *"let's do a pricing study".* Immediately after *all,* an increase in selling price *goes* straight to the best *line.*

By carrying out *the* study you could acquire useful data on the impact of a possible improve, however, you *also* could *be blindsided by* contemplating that the market *variables* you will be evaluating *are* unbiased *from other* sector *variables.* Such as accomplishing *a pricing* analyze by itself won't consider *the* effect on product layout, competitive *positioning, segments,* marketing *channels, or other* critical features of the promoting system. *Nor* does it supply you with *the correlations (*bring about *and* outcome*)* between each of the internet marketing elements, *nor the* underlying current market drivers that outline the marketplace traits that you choose to will have to handle *to* grow your business. A lot more essential, it could *not* properly handle *the* competitive reaction to creating *a* alter in any *or* most of the internet marketing *variables.*

Anything you really need to have *is* current market *intelligence, the* seize *of* many of the suitable market place details which has been built-in, *analyzed, and interpreted* specifically *to* much more fully consider all your options *for* advancement. Current market *intelligence* not simply recognizes *the interference* from the 4 *P's (*Products, Marketing, Selling price *and* Position*); but* products *that interdependence* in a very *way* that allows you to definitely take into consideration various choices and also the affiliate possibility.

An efficient industry *intelligence* effort demands the marketplace crew *to:*

1. Know what you will need. Generally *this* phase *is taken* with no consideration provided *the* team *ongoing* discussions; even so it is actually essential to grasp exactly what the *intelligence* will be to *be use for, to* recognize what on earth is required. Dependent on "*what* it will require *to* get," establish approach options *and* challenges *that* want to generally be resolved. *From this* do the job they could quickly describe whatever they required to *know* to transform *hypotheses into* sector strategy.

2. Understand what info *to* capture. Below it really is greatest to get started on that has a *blank slate.* Along with the *strategic* objectives in your mind, an inventory *of* critical challenges has to *be* dealt with. *These* consist of aggressive *positioning,* value of factors, critical outcomes, *pricing,* purchaser *attitudes, and* difficulties. A few of the things of such need to by now *been* regarded, *but some* may still *be* concealed.

3. Layout *your* awareness seize method. *The* 3 vital steps here *are:*

· Believe *'outcomes' or* just what the *specifies* from the market place may want to transpire for a result of *an* conversation along with you. *They* get services and products that can help *them get their* employment done.

· *Do a qualitative* market place evaluation *to* recognize *the* concealed aspects *and validate* the list *of* opportunity results *are* correct. The main element right here should be to find *what specifies* price along with the criteria *they use to* measure supplier efficiency.

· Design and style *your quantitative* sector study inside a *way* that you *can* both measure the industry *and* test ideas. A superb *quantitative* layout *employs* exercises where *the respondent is* asked to generate options *on* what on earth is critical *to them and identifies* the problem *a respondent is* getting *in* accomplishing *their* primary results. The design must seize *the respondents' beliefs and attitudes* concerning the main subject matter, aggressive actions, *and willingness to* act as desired.

four. *Compile the learning's* -- and obtain the entire story. *A well-*

designed market place *intelligence* examine should give you *'causal' or prescriptive* watch from the industry. *These learning's* should really *be translated into actionable implications. A* important benefit *to this* tactic *is* models *that* allow *your* group to carry out *'What if' analyses.*

With out delivering *actionable implications,* market *intelligence* is sort of useless. One particular corporation *complained* a great deal of concerning the high quality in their *quantitative* marketplace research they *stopped* performing *surveys* altogether. In their terms, nothing *was actionable.* Nevertheless having a distinctive method of gaining sector *intelligence,* and also a method to create *off of qualitative learning's an actionable* method *was* located.

5. Offer several *perceptions* in the marketplace. The industry is composed of various groups of consumers, which can be generally known as *segments. These segments* might may perhaps *be* situated in distinctions *in* key sector motorists such *by* consequence overall performance, *attitudes,* and have advantages, in addition *as slicing by* vital *demographic and* sales factors. *By segmenting on behavioral* components, you are able to equally determine several price *propositions* and choose goal teams *that* finest in shape *your* functionality to deliver value. Analysis *by* segment *also* informs you how you *fare* from levels of competition inside of every single team.

In one case in point, a company observed *that with two* from the four recognized *segments* they might deliver exclusive benefit *propositions* to each much better *than their* rivals *could.* Once identified, *they then* observed a way to interact every single of those *two segments uniquely modifying all* factors of their marketing blend including *pricing selectively* to every, as well as in different ways *than* to the *non-targeted segments.*

6. Produce *and* test persuasive options. Successful industry *intelligence* should really create *the* opportunity *for* different techniques. *Your* group ought to have *some hypotheses about* alternatives before *embarking* right into a sector *intelligence* analyze. Those alternatives need to *be* analyzed during the *qualitative* stage; *then* built to the *quantitative* analyze. *In*

compiling the learning, and attaining *the* multiple *perceptions,* you may deliver *analytics on* just about every alternative *and* conduct danger *assessments.*

In one illustration, a company located a possible *new* prospect, *a "Blue Ocean,"* which was over and above the original *scope* of their market *intelligence. They went* again to the market to test *the* ensuing worth *proposition with* likely *early adopters* for a *new* system. The result *that drove them to reevaluate was "We want our* supplier *to 'take charge'* from the complete *transaction. They* were initially unwilling to include *that* outcome. After *explored* even more, *they* had been in a position *to validate* the result *and* build a value *proposition* which they *could* deliver against. *This* elevated *their* base *line* by means of financial state *of scale.*

A marketplace *intelligence* analyze *incorporates* an extensive evaluation *and* analysis with the significant elements of your business enterprise interaction by using a described marketplace. Naturally the look depends to the character of one's industry as well as the aggressive atmosphere. Nonetheless for some business enterprise *to* business enterprise markets, *the* examine should really be able industry *intelligence* to answer *most* or even every one of these concerns:

· *How* critical *our* product or service attributes towards the market and the way *do* the main competition *(*including *us)* perform against these characteristics?

· *What* rewards *(*outcomes*) do the specifying* customers in the market place would like to achieve and the way *do they* perceive *their* major *suppliers* accomplishing *relative to* those outcomes?

· *How can we distinguish* amongst *what* prospects *say* is essential and how they really *behave vs. their* stated great importance?

· How do *these* attributes *and* results vary *by* different *segments* from the market, *or what segments are derived from* distinct *responses to attribute and* end result significance?

· *How will* selling price variations impression aggressive *share* and how *does that* vary among the *the* outlined *segments* based upon *attribute and* end result relevance?

· Exactly what is the right stability amongst cost *and share that maximizes our* gains?

· *How would* shoppers worth a whole new products notion *that* we've been contemplating *bringing* for the industry *and what would they be* ready to pay with the idea?

· *How would* shoppers price *some new* offering attributes *we* may possibly convey for the market place, and the way *does that* worth differ through the prospects?

· *What new* options would offer *us* using a *'blue ocean' of* option?

· How can buyers understand *our* brand name *vs.* competitive models?

· Exactly what are *the* underlying *structural* elements *and attitudes* of the industry *which* define wherever we need *to* aim *for* potential progress?

CHAPTER 3

QUANTITATIVE, QUALITATIVE OR HYBRID - THINK OUT OF BOX INNOVATION THAT LEADS TO INSIGHTFUL OUTCOMES

In case you *hope to* constantly improve your enterprise *and* contend from the *new* world marketplace, you will need to be capable of properly approach *and execute a strategic* advertising strategy *cost-effectively and* by using a concentration *on Return On* Financial commitment *(ROI)*.

Regrettably, numerous modest entrepreneurs *and solopreneurs* sign up for *the ranks* of your *self-employed* with out a robust knowledge of your *fundamentals of strategic* marketing, as an alternative getting *a "see what comes"* tactic, *which invariably* potential customers *to lower-than-expected* final results and it is an enormous *contributing* variable during the *stratospheric* rate of latest business enterprise *failures*.

To help you you plan *your strategic* marketing and advertising method, here i will discuss *the* seven Actions *To* Developing *A Concise* Tiny Company Marketing Strategy*:*

Stage 1*:* Make a Advertising and marketing Eyesight

Would you know very well what you happen to be seeking to carry out using your marketing initiatives*; what your* precise targets *are* on the subject of escalating *and* making your small business*?* Knowledge in which you *are and* realizing in which you need to *go* would be the necessary initial step *to* producing *an* motion strategy to have *you there*.

Stage2*:* Fully grasp *Your* Current market

That's *your* excellent shopper *or* consumer*?* Would you *know or* are you only willing to acquire *any* small business *that* comes *your way?* Having the ability to determine, realize *and empathize* together with your probable shoppers *will* exhibit *to them* which you can *relate to them* and are truly worried about delivering *them* an answer that actually works *for them*.

Being able to *"speak the language"* of one's potential client will allow you to achieve *their* trust *and* build *rapport* considerably more speedily, ultimately top *to* greater accomplishment.

Stage 3*: Know Your* Competitors

What do your opponents *do* effectively*? What do* they do poorly*? How will you differentiate* oneself *from them* inside the *minds* of the future shoppers*?*

Doing the best forms *of* competitive assessment, together with getting to be *a* buyer within your competitiveness making sure that you already know *first-hand* what they present and the way well *or* improperly *they* supply to the *sale.*

It is possible to discover quite a bit with regards to their buyer services, shipping and delivery approaches, merchandise *pricing & quality and* way more *by* getting *their* purchaser. You could *also find out if* and how *they continue to* current market *to you after the initial sale has been completed.*

Stage *4: Craft A Compelling Message*

Once you realize *what your* objectives *are, have a clear* understanding *of what the* current market *wants, what is important to them and what holes* you can *fill* while in the market place *by* executing *a complete* aggressive examination, you'll be able to *then craft a compelling* marketing and advertising *message to clearly and concisely convey the benefits* of the assistance *offering.*

Your message should always be benefit-driven and speak *directly to the emotional wants and needs* of the possible buyers. *Your goal is to answer the two most important questions before they are ever asked: 'what's so good about that?'; and 'what's in it for me?"*

Finally, your message should illicit a response. Gone would be the *days when getting "exposure" (also known as branding) is enough to ensure your* good results. *Today,* you need to *be focused on* promoting attempts *that generate an immediate result so* you can effectively *gauge your return on* expense.

Stage *5: Selecting Message Delivery Systems*

There are thousands (or rather, tens and even hundreds of

thousands) of different ways you may sector *your message* during the *attempt to reach your* current market; *however* several *of them will be ineffective at best.*

Using your buyer *profile,* you'll be able to *begin to do research on how to reach your prospects* during the *places they are already spending time. There's no point in advertising in a magazine for dogs to promote your cat training system!*

Does one would like to *advertise* during the *paper, online or through direct-mail? What about yellow pages, white papers or trade publications? How about* additional *"guerrilla" style* internet marketing *such as staged events, public relations or street-teams?*

There are too quite a few *options to list and it is your job to determine* the right *ones to reach your* market during the *most cost-effective way possible.*

Stage *6: Tracking Your* Outcomes

How will you know *whether your* promoting endeavors *are successful or whether* you're simply *throwing good money after bad by renewing a losing campaign? Tracking your* attempts is usually a *key component, made easier by* using *a direct-response* approach with the internet marketing *campaigns.*

Using unique tracking codes (and requesting this information at the point of sale) will help you *know* the place your organization *is coming from* to ensure you may *track your conversions appropriately.*

Having buyers clip a coupon, quote a VIP Access Code or type in a precise *website address for each different campaign are all simple ways* you could *begin to track the effectiveness* within your internet marketing *with the goal of* accomplishing much more *of what* is effective *and less of what doesn't.*

Step seven*:* Building Internet marketing *Systems*

Once you have a advertising prepare *in place that is working, how will you automate or systemize it* to ensure that it is possible to *become even* a lot more *effective* together with your *time, getting* additional *and better* outcomes *while putting in less human effort?*

By building *a funnel* solution *to your* promoting *you will* have the capacity to produce a *sense of continuity from one level* on the *funnel to the next. Not only will your clients feel* much more *comfortable along each* stage, *you will also know how to respond or what* action *to* take *whenever you have an interaction with that* customer, *based on* exactly where *they are* from the *funnel process you've developed*

CHAPTER 4

MODES OF INTERVIEWING

The merchandise of information collected given that the basis of promoting exploration are generally generally known as facts *and we* speak *of* key information *and secondary* knowledge. The former *is* info gathered by means of *a* analysis *program* completed for your unique reason. *The latter is* data *that* previously *exists,* because it *was* collected *as* portion of *a* earlier exploration procedure *or* for a few distinctive objective.

Secondary information are available within a firm, *in* revenue records in particular. *When* useful for marketing and advertising study, this kind of information probably will need *reorganizing.* As an example, revenue of a specific product or service *will* usually *be* stated buyer *by* client, whereas *the* investigate may call for the *geographical breakdown. Alternatively,* several exterior resources *of secondary* info can be found, *in* authorities *departments, trade associations,* professional *bodies, the* press, expert research companies and a lot of *other* resources. *The* rising *availability,* electric power and adaptability *of* pcs will make *it* more and more effortless *for this* data being produced straight away available to conclusion *makers.* An increasing array *of databases can now be accessed on-line.*

Some investigation agencies work *syndicated* exploration *program in* specific *fields.* These are definitely investigation *program* build on a *co-operative* basis *and* paid *for by contributions from* each individual with the providers collaborating. Normally it is achievable *to 'buy into'* such *a program* and therefore obtain obtain *to* facts already collected. *Alternatively,* businesses sometimes *mount a program of* exploration *and* give the outcomes available for sale *to* anyone intrigued. *Trade associations* often make sure details *freely* accessible to *their* members *but* promote *it to 'outsiders'.*Progressively all this type of facts *is* crafted right into a complete *'Marketing* Information and facts *System'* that is constantly *up-dated.*Identifying suitable resources *of secondary* data, *extracting the* applicable data *and analysing* it is actually usually known as *desk* study.

The gathering *of* Most important Data

If your data needed to get a certain marketing study task won't already *exist as secondary* knowledge, we now have to find out the simplest way *of* accumulating *it.* You will discover three elementary strategies for the selection *of* primary facts - *observation, experiment, and* study. It's the 3rd tactic that many persons generally affiliate *with* market place analysis. The primary *two,* nevertheless, also have an important position *to* perform *in* selected conditions.

Observation

It can be often far better to view *what* men and women *do* instead of *to* ask *them* what they *do. This has the* gain *that it* gets rid of *any* difficulty *of interviewer-bias and avoids* the problem that men and women tend not to normally try to remember *their* steps - in particular *trivial* ones - very clearly. For example, *a* concealed camera may be the greatest technique for developing *how* shoppers shift through a shop, and also a *tape recorder* the most beneficial technique of developing *the* product sales method used by *salesmen.* In the same way *a* bodily depend is often employed to establish the volume *of* traffic *on* crucial streets as well as the quantity of various brands sold *by* vital shops *(*ever more by way of digital place *of sale - EPOS - installations).*

Experiment

Simulation of a authentic scenario may well typically be a much better technique for examining possible future behavior *than* inquiring people *hypothetical* thoughts. It really is *notoriously* tricky to *get* dependable solutions *about* doable long run behaviour*; but, if* one example is, we would like to understand *which of two* possible deals *housewives* would prefer, we can easily place *them* aspect *by* side in the authentic *or dummy* shop, give a team *of housewives a* browsing list *and* funds to invest and see *which pack they* opt for. Equally, a means *of* evaluating children's choice *for* a person *toy as* towards an additional will be to provide a team of kids *a 'selection of toys to* engage in *with* and find out *what* happens *(*just how during which *they* play can also generate worthwhile *insights).* Test promoting *is* obviously *an* example of *experiments* to be a usually means *of* acquiring advertising research facts.

Fundamental Forms *of* Study

If it is required to acquire most important information *by* study, a few solutions can be obtained. They are really *(a)* individual *interviews, (b)* telephone *interviews, and (c) postal questionnaires.* Generally speaking, the fee *decreases as we go down this* checklist, *but so does the* reliability and also the *extent* from the information that may *be* received.Particular *interviewing* is among the most flexible and can reasonably quickly *be* carried out on the basis of the appropriately chosen *sample.* Numerous in depth questions is often requested, and the responses is often *supplemented* through the *interviewer's* particular *observations if* essential. Though the cost for each *interviewer is* high, and also the degree *of* scheduling *and supervision* necessary adds even more on the price.

Telephone *interviewing* permits many individuals to get reached rapidly about a wide *geographical* location. For this reason it really is broadly utilized *in industrial* internet marketing exploration. *Its* negatives *are that,* generally speaking, *only* small *interviews* of the *impersonal* character can be carried out. Answers can be *keyed straight in for* laptop or computer evaluation, supplying more cost *reductions.*

Postal questionnaires are relatively pretty low-priced. However, *the* reaction price *(*number of people that *return* thoroughly done *questionnaires)* will likely be pretty small, *which introduces its* have method of *bias.*

Other Study Techniques

For individual uses, versions of your subsequent *surveying* approaches *have proved* valuable.

Panels

When continuing analysis is required, *the panel* technique is usually employed. *This differs* within the advert *hoc enquiry in* which the identical team *(or panel) of informants is* used to offer *a* series of answers above *a* duration of *time. This arrangement* is particularly precious when the want is usually to set up traits. Shortcomings *are* that it's hard to keep more than an extended period of time *a panel* that is really agent*; panel* customers may possibly little by little turn into *self-conscious* as well as data they provide now not *a spontaneous expression* in their personalized sights. *Panels are* employed extensively *in listener/viewer* study and the *retail* shop *audit panel* is a properly founded supply of data.

Discussion Groups

A little *(*ordinarily all over 8*)* and punctiliously picked group of individuals *are* brought together to debate a selected matter. *The interviewer* does not generally *pose* distinct inquiries *but intervenes only* to make certain that *the* discussion *stays on* matter and that *all* important factors *are* talked about. Due to the fact *interpretation of* results is usually hard, *interviewers (*or more properly discussion *leaders) are* commonly skilled *psychologists.*

Discussion groups simply cannot *be* considered adequately representative *and statistical* examination is often unattainable. Nonetheless, they may have *the* gain *that (a)* they are relatively reasonably priced, *and (b) the dynamic* team condition may deliver *out* information that could *not* happen to be *foreseen by* an individual developing *a questionnaire. The* strategy is especially useful *in* obtaining info promptly *and inexpensively, e.g.* as a information *to copywriters and* item advancement teams *and* as an aid *in* setting up *questionnaires for pilot surveys.*

Motivational Analysis

This experienced a solid *vogue some* a long time back *but* is currently significantly less well-known. *It* works by using procedures tailored *from* medical *psychology* in an try to determine *motives for* conduct *and* opinions. *The* approaches made use of involve word association, *ink-blot* exams, *and sentence completion* assessments.

CHAPTER 5

PROS & CONS OF DIVERSE TECHNOLOGY AND FIELD CHANNELS ENHANCING PROJECT ROI

Your sample ought to *be* agent from the inhabitants being a full.

Your goal group is not really Internet *oriented and/or* may not *have an E-Mail* deal with *or* world wide web relationship, *as* in a very modest company, and so forth.,

You don't have *Opt-In E-Mail addresses,* however you *do have* telephone numbers.

You will need *to* monitor for your distinct person within a organization, *i.e. the VP of Finance.*

You may have an extremely lengthy *or* extremely complicated study that may *also* have to have *a* reside *interviewer for prompting, clarification and probing.*

You might have several open ended inquiries.

You've got a little *sample* dimension *(10-30)* that could *not justify the programming* fees.

You might have *to* identify the person *by* phone, display *them* and possess only a few inquiries *to* question; as a result *it* saves time and money to easily talk to *the* thoughts whilst you might have *them* over the phone

Causes *for Conducting* an online *or* World-wide-web Centered Study:

You have already got *a* consumer list *or Opt-In E-mail* listing, which would necessarily mean *$$* could be *saved in* obtaining *no* phone *recruiting* value.

Your concentrate on team *is* World wide web *savvy, has E-Mail addresses* and is particularly *accustomed to* applying the web.

Your concentrate on group includes a higher interested in collaborating *i.e. membership lists.*

You might have *a graphic,* strategy *or presentation* that might *be* seen quickly over a web site thereby conserving the expense *and time of printing and postage.*

A visible *presentation* from the inquiries themselves could well be less complicated to understand *than* listening to *the* questions *(audio).*

You desire *them* to give you lengthy comprehensive answers *to* open up finished questions. Take note: you'll unfastened the aid *of probing* approaches.

You would like specified forms of facts; confidential, embarrassing *or* information they could *not have* readily available *to them.*

You've got *a* tracking analyze that could continue for any duration of time permitting the online study to just not sleep and be employed *indefinitely,* thereby saving *new* set up *and programming* costs.

Pluses & Minuses of Net *Research:*

Eight Pluses:

1-Respondents can complete the survey *at their leisure.*

2-Respondents often use a *higher interest in* collaborating, *once they agree.*

3-Speed -- 90% of results arrive within the first 2 days ? 30% - 50% in the first number of *hours!*

4-Geographical issues: respondents can be local or world wide.

5-Costs can be lower but not always.

6-Can be easier *to find* specific *hard to find respondents.*

7-Relative anonymity of the Net *and* Internet *customs* might *produce more* detailed, *thoughtful, honest* responses *which they might be reluctant to tell an interviewer in* particular person.

8-Many more persons are on-line *today.*

Eight Minuses:

1-Relative anonymity can produce more conveniently *expresses negative* answers*!*

2-Requires careful screening to verify respondents are who they say they are.

3-Sample isn't *project able and* as a result *is more qualitative than quantitative in nature.*

4-Length of respondent's attention for focus groups (45 minutes) is more limited than during an in man or woman group *as respondents can just wander away from their computers!*

5-Size of on-line *focus groups* should *be somewhat smaller (6-8) in order to handle the* group *and allow all to participate.*

6-Typos and spelling errors are an undeniable part of communicating to the Net*!*

7-Although greatly improved, use on the World wide web *can sometimes be challenging in that lines can unexpectedly go down and there is nothing you can do about it but wait or re-schedule.*

8-If respondents are not Web *savvy they will* have to *be educated and coached through the process, this can be a challenge!*

About Return rates for Email Studies and Web-based Surveys

The following facts *all assumes that respondents have either agreed to participate through a* telephone *recruit or are members of a* group, enterprise *or association, or are a* customer *of such* group, enterprise *or association.*

The return rate for the blanket outreach of email just isn't much different than a mail study where return rate can be 10%.

Return rates for email invitations to go to an online primarily based survey, are generally less than 10% depending around the specifics of your analyze.

The following all affect return rates:

1)How serious about general are they in the topic?

2)Is an incentive offered and how much?

3)Duration of survey.

4)Fits into your schedule. In general the setup takes the most time but the speed in the return rate is fast. 90% in first 48 hours, almost all within a week.

Pointers for Conducting an online Dependent study:

Dependent on my 18 years like a Field Director and my a lot of years of developing on-line surveys and projects, these are the things clients should know. With all this said and done, Online Research is an exciting new opportunity to gather data in ways the Marketing Research Industry could have never anticipated and has lots of as yet unexplored avenues.

Usually do not assume because it is going with a computer that anything can be done. Use the KISS philosophy. Simple gets better results and expenditures less.

Net programming takes time, anywhere from a couple of days to a week to program and test. Strategy this into your schedule. In general the set up takes the most time but the speed with the return rate is fast. 90% in first 48 hours, almost all within a week.

Make sure your questionnaire is final before giving to the programmer; changes take money and time and can delay the start date.

You may perhaps *think your draft questionnaire is shorter than it really is. It is hard* for just a client *to estimate the* duration *of a* study based on a *Word document that, yes indeed,* may perhaps *occupy one page in* size. *Each question* which could *be within a question has* to generally be *separated out and asked individually. Don't be surprised when your 2 page word doc turns into 50* inquiries*! Best to* talk to *ONLY actionable "necessary"* concerns *and not "nice to know" type of* issues.

There is no "magic number" of issues *to* ask within a world wide web survey, *like 6* issues *or 15* issues = ten *minutes for* duration of your time *for respondents to complete the* survey. *Keep* issues *as brief and simple and actionable as possible. Then submit your draft questionnaire to your supplier for an evaluation of* size of your time.

Open up finished queries, *like: What do you think of our recent changes? Are more expensive to tab and code, as opposed to a* list *closed* ended answers, *like: Which* on the *following best describes your opinion on our recent changes? Check one: ()* Very *satisfied, () Somewhat satisfied,* and many others. *To keep* prices *down keep* open up finished inquiries *to a minimum unless they are really what* you need *and are willing to pay the coding* expenditures.

You can show graphics and collateral's conveniently inside a *web-based* study, *but it will* will need *some preparation. Remember though, it is being* considered over a *computer* screen *and* hence *does not have the quality of a printed document and has to meet size/download speed requirements. In my experience, graphics always* have to have *some work before they can be shown* over a *website. A Power Point document cannot be considered* to get *of good enough quality to go directly to* a web *graphic! Nor is one that is printer ready and* features a *huge file* measurement. *Know that your supplier will* must *tweak the graphic.*

About "templates": You may possibly *have been given what someone told you was a "template" and you* might *have been given the impression this would then make the* study a lot easier *and less costly. A "template" is a "survey" that someone else has done with their software and their system requirements. For them it is a template. For your supplier it is someone else's programming that we will* must *re-program - in the worst case - or re-use pieces of in the best case.*

Price tag *factor: You* could *have heard that* net *surveys are* quite *cheap or* price tag *less. This can be true, but that depends entirely on who your respondent is, how* effortlessly *he can be recruited, the* duration from the survey, *complexity of* study *and the return rate factors listed.* Will not *just assume* a web *base* study *will be automatically cheaper.*

CHAPTER 6

COST EFFECTIVE ONLINE SURVEY SOLUTIONS

Properly, almost.... *Not all* on the internet survey software organizations *will* match your specific needs. You are going to require to shop all around. On-line survey software program corporations *all* give study *creators,* data selection, and many related capabilities. *How, then, are* business enterprise individuals intended to make a decision *which* software fits *their* requires finest? Study creation is essential mainly because it affects *what respondents* experience during *their* survey *and* decides *drop-out* concentrations. It is actually critical to remember *the* get in touch with management of your software package: *what* attributes *exist for publishing surveys?* When you collect facts then you most likely have to have *to* present the outcomes and so *the reporting* capabilities on the program are also important. *With* all of these attributes readily available, *we could* opt for anyone of these *to* foundation *our* conclusion *on. This* choice relies upon with your as well as your *business'* needs.

1 strategy to make a selection, which may prove most effective *for* identifying *the utility* of the computer software to your company, is usually to position much more significance over the info examination abilities from the numerous software program firms. To get meaningful benefits out of your study you require a lot more than *just* figures *and percentages.* You would like state-of-the-art details evaluation. Advanced knowledge assessment involves making use of *multi-level crosstabs* to obtain brand name responses, such as. A different case in point may be *conducting pricing* investigation *to* measure *the* chance *of* acquire at a unique cost level. To supply *you with* small business remedies survey software package needs to *go* previously mentioned *and* further than straightforward survey creation *and* facts collection. Highly developed knowledge evaluation *is* crucial.

You can find much prospective *for* study application to offer authentic small business solutions. It is significant for you plus your business enterprise to look for *the* characteristics *in* each business that will most effective match your requirements. Here are a few of your options that could deliver possible answers for your personal company:

Options *for* internet marketing*:*
On-line study program *has the* probable to help you to realize *your* present *and* foreseeable future markets making use of assessment *to* id very clear action details *that feed into* marketing and advertising options. Specific study software package firms hold the probable to become significant market place study resources on your organization. *By capturing* shopper comments you could make certain that *you* minimize buyer *churn* to develop associations *and* retain customers happy. You may also analyze study information to hurry *up* a completely new products development process *and* assemble feed-back from the target industry *on pricing, new* product or service ideas *and* merchandise capabilities. *By* amassing feedback *on* promotion concepts, website design, *packaging, logos, etcetera,* you can increase recent advertising strategies *and fine-tune* foreseeable future ones. Such as, *some* program allows you to *use multi-level cross-tabulations* to acquire brand name opinions *from* numerous *populations;* test advertising principles working with *heat-map or* movie*; and* conduct *pricing* examination *with scale slider* questions to measure *the* probability *of* invest in at a distinct value place. *This* computer software *even* enables you to make *multilingual surveys* so as assemble world-wide responses from the shoppers everywhere in the globe.

Options *for* sales*:*
Applying online *surveys* it is possible to capture useful customer comments to offer data in your Product sales department about their current pleasure *and dissatisfaction* ranges in addition *as* foreseeable future needs. *Use this* information and facts *to* recognize *'at-risk'* buyers, *follow-up on* brings about acquire *new* organization *or upsell to* prospects who've *unfulfilled* prerequisites. *Use* craze analysis *to* measure variations *in* shopper feedback with time. Applying advanced investigation features *to* detect apparent action details *that feed into* revenue strategy *can* optimize *your business'* associations *with* shoppers. You'll be able to examine *the* impact *of* advertising campaigns among *your* profits *forces. Some* organizations *make* items a little bit less complicated *by funneling* study info directly to *your* product sales crew *with Sales force integration.* By doing this *your* Product sales section *is alerted to dissatisfied* prospects *and* presents the opportunity to create

associations before the shopper *dissatisfaction reaches* significant levels.

Solutions *for Human* Resources*:*
They backbone of your business enterprise may be the people today *who* ensure it is operate*: your* staff members. *To* enhance your company you need to make sure *your* group *is* healthy, content, *and* effective. Study computer software can offer revolutionary remedies *to* retaining *your* group satisfied *and* performing at the highest in their sport. Using online *surveys* it is possible to obtain feed-back *from* workers *about* company communication, rewards, *salaries,* pleasure, education *and* improvement alternatives. *With* attributes these kinds of *as 'grouping'* you could produce *360-degree* feed-back *from questionnaires, e-learning quizzes* or maybe *post-training* tests. *The* responses you get will enable you to improve *churn* premiums, boost internal *communications,* tackle spots of upper *dissatisfaction, and* establish ideal education systems. The probabilities *for* collecting suggestions *are* limitless, *but* obviously, once more, you will need to *use* instruments *with* highly developed knowledge assessment to deal with *this* details effectively.

Each individual organization is seeking approaches to enhance *their* income, fulfill *their* customers, *and* preserve *their* staff joyful. On-line study program *is* one particular approach to supply your enterprise *with* alternatives *and* tools to obtain *these* goals. It is important to search for interesting survey *creators to* improve *respondent* experience *and* boost *your* probabilities of getting extra *responses.* Even so, *as* I have emphasized in this post it's the details evaluation factors of your computer software *that* offer by far the most rewards *and* answers on your organization. There are plenty of survey program organizations *that* supply these types of data analysis tools. You must shop all around *a* locate the tool that suits *your* distinct desires. Engage *in* intelligent *consumerism,* transcend *the* survey *sending* step, *and* desire more from your survey tools.

CHAPTER 7

COACHING YOUR CLIENTS HELPING THEM UNDERSTAND THEIR CUSTOMER'S PROFILE FOCUSING DEMOGRAPHICS

Like every small business proprietor *or* supervisor, you would probably enjoy *to* increase your organization, convey *in new* consumers, and find out current shoppers improve *their* exercise along with you. Buyer *profiling* is actually a crucial stage into the effective *and* efficient advertising within your organization.

You can find *two* most important strategies *of profiling your* shoppers:

1) *Mining* information and facts *you* previously obtain while in the day *to* day action of your respective business *and,*

2) *Conducting* current market investigate amongst consumers *and* probable marketplaces

The primary move *in profiling* is always to just take a tough glance *at your customers'* business along with you. You will be wanting to answer thoughts such as:

--*Who are my* best buyers?

--*What are my* best clients getting?

--*How* extensive *have they been* obtaining *from my* corporation?

--*How* prolonged *did it* get *them* to become *my* most effective buyers?

Performing this is fairly straightforward.

You team *your* shoppers *by their* value to you personally. Select an inexpensive *time horizon,* like one year. Add *up* the whole income *by* shopper in excess of *this* time period. *Now* different the outcome *into* groups. Normally you'll discover the *80/20 rule applies* in this article, at the very least roughly. *Some 20%* within your prospects *(or 15% to 25%) will* offer you *80%* of one's profits *(or 70% to 90%).* The secret is in order to glimpse especially with the team of shoppers that are most significant to you personally.

You must *know* in addition *what your* subsequent *"best"* group of consumers *are* performing, and so forth, right down to *your occasional or* rare customers. You would look in the *longevity* of the shoppers in the identical style. Take *your* most valuable customer group *and* look *at their* background along with you. *Have they* generally *been your* most useful customers? Just how long ended up *they* shoppers prior to *they moved into this* group? How much business enterprise *did* they are doing with you right up until *they* achieved *this* position?

You'll *also* search for the mix of services and products your best clients had been acquiring and exactly how routinely. *Do they* buy a tiny at a *time, but* accomplish that often? *Or do they* obtain all of sudden? You'll be able to do this *with* every single of one's revenue groups.

You now know which customers *are* critical to the business. In case you contain the info *internally,* you'd probably seem *also* on the *demographic profiles* of the profits teams.

--*What are their ages?*

--*How* very well *educated (or not) are they?*

--*What is their* profits stage?

--*How are they* utilized?

In the event you don't have *this* data, you could possibly perform current market study together with your shoppers to understand. *This* details gives you a robust advertising *arsenal.* Understanding *who* your best buyers *are,* you should learn to *migrate other* buyers you've *into this* team. Working with current market investigation equipment such as *surveys* or just getting conversations with your very best shoppers can offer lots of *insights into why* they are doing organization with you.

Soon after *all,* it's *a truism* that it is a great deal more highly-priced *to* go out *and* look for a *new* prospects *than* it is actually to better services *your* current clients to make sure that they are really captivated to do far more small business along with you.

Customer *profiling* assists *you* produce promoting campaigns that speak instantly to each group within your prospects. *And with* industry investigation, you can realize the things they *see* because the rewards *of* accomplishing small business along with you. You'll be able to *then* support grow income from the existing client base *and by* being familiar with the advantages *your* latest clients *derive from* executing enterprise with you, you should utilize people added benefits *to* industry effectively for brand spanking new prospective buyers.

CHAPTER 8

HOW INTUITION HELPS YOU DEVELOP COMMENDABLE INSIGHTS FOR YOUR FINAL REPORT

Every year providers expend many pounds *on* sector analysis, trying to be familiar with *what* buyers *want* in order to most effective fulfill those people wishes by *the* firm's offerings. Having said that, *in* making an attempt to comprehend what will fulfill shopper would like, businesses often concentrate *their* sector study only to the requires *expressed by customers-the "voice of customer" in* marketing and advertising *jargon. But voice of* client *only captures expressed* wants, *not* every one of the true customer wants available in the market. *By* implementing instinct *to* current market study, entrepreneurs have the ability to far more absolutely have an understanding of the particular consumer demands while in the marketplace, also to thereby comprehend *a* aggressive *edge in* gratifying shoppers *and* generating gross sales.

Even though industry investigation is definitely an invaluable resource *for* mastering *the expressed* requires from the buyer, current market investigation *can only* capture wants which the client will be able to *articulate.* In truth, individuals usually do not constantly know what they need, *and statistical* industry facts, *or* emphasis teams, can't reveal *what* customers them selves do not know. *The* Weather conditions *Channel* is usually a great illustration. Inside the *1980's,* interest *in* information regarding the climate *was* imagined to get *strictly local--market* analysis had revealed that buyers needed neighborhood weather *reporting. But* a little group received the concept that *a 24 hour* climate *channel would* arrive at *a* industry *of* shoppers *that resonated* with the providing *of regional and* countrywide weather conditions furthermore *to* area weather conditions. Despite of *what* conventional current market analysis and traditional thinking *held, the* Weather *Channel* now is usually a *multi-million* dollar *cable channel* company with an *accompanying* internet site *that* receives around 300 *million* once-a-year views.

The background *of* markets *has* demonstrated *that* clients will not be fantastic *at expressing* requires *for visionary* offerings *not* but *in existence.* Such as, merchandise *in* widespread *use* these days, like the computer, *the* iPhone, *or chunky pasta sauce, all* took place by means of *the visionary* instinct in their *inventors. The existence* of the market for every *of* these *new* products and solutions *was envisioned* by *the* instinct from the *marketer, not* via standard current market study solutions. *In essence,* probably the most successful internet marketing views traditional sector exploration by way of *the lens of* instinct.

But how can you need to do *that?* See classic industry exploration by means of *the lens of* instinct? How could you *use* industry analysis *and* instinct to establish whether *the "next* greatest *thing"* that you are making are going to be recognized from the market place? The 1st area to get started on *is with* very good, strong, common *research-your* instinct has got to *have* facts to work *with,* as well as your firm needs to *have* logical causes *why the* internet marketing need to function. *But what then?* Allow *me* clarify *by recounting what I did.*

During *my time* with a *Fortune* 500 enterprise, I was charged with the responsibility *for* industry *intelligence.* It was *my* position *to* carry out market exploration about the firm's *new* products and solutions, to investigate *that* exploration, also to build a method *for* successfully internet marketing these solutions, every one of the although remaining aware *of* exactly what the firm's competition have been possible to perform in the very same sector. Numerous facts *was* obtainable *to me-from* financial investment banking institutions *to* specialized investigate corporations. Other folks having a position *like mine* during the company's *other divisions* experienced *an* precision amount of approximately *70% in predicting what* opponents *would do and* if they *would* get it done. *But my* accuracy charge *was way* better, shut *to 95%. When senior* administration *concluded that my* accuracy level *was* as a result of the quantity of information *and* examination methods I was working with, the corporate *synthesized my* investigate equipment *and* investigation procedures into a method *for other divisions* to implement, *but their* final results have been never ever far better as opposed to typical *70%.*

The actual solution *to my* achievement charge *was to* read through *the voluminous* promoting facts, and after that to employ *my* instinct *to* go beyond *it.* By way of example, once the process *was* to analyze *what a competitor's* steps in a very sector *would* very likely *be,* I'd normally begin *by* researching the data, which might produce *some* solutions *but* by no means *the breakthrough* response that was worthy of *basing a* trustworthy tactic *on.* Soon after *my* study *was* total, I might talk to *my* instinct exactly where to search for the data that would *reliably* predict long run *competitor* exercise. Focusing on the standard promoting details I had currently examined, *my* intuition *would* normally occur *through--I would* frequently get a authentic intestine experience *that* explained to *me* which i experienced hit the best information and facts *stream.* I'd personally *then* adhere to *that* gut sensation *to hypothesize what* motion *the competitor would* probably choose. It absolutely was *my* gut experience *that* permitted *me to go from* a median *analyst* to at least one *that* regularly produced near *flawless predictions about competitor moves 2-3* many years later on. *What* would it *be* worth to you personally *or* your organization to know *your* rivals *moves* to the following *2-3* many years?

Working with *your* instinct to comprehend sector study is really a terrific blend *that* qualified prospects to some real knowledge of the marketplace. *This* potent *one-two punch* could make *you* dollars, help save *you* money, and provides *you a* internet marketing edge *that* knowledge by itself will never *give your* level of competition.

CHAPTER 9

HOW TO WRITE WINNING PROPOSALS

We are *concentrating on* getting ready *proposals in* reaction to your Request *for Proposal (RFP)* from the Govt. Agency. The main component, *Introduction, addresses the RFP, its* make-up, and the *accompanying "Instructions to Offers".*

Introduction

Creating *a* profitable *proposal* is almost *trivial,* a minimum of *the* producing element. The general approach *of* making ready *and presenting a proposal* which will get *a* agreement is more difficult, extra *formidable,* and much more challenging *than* could possibly be anticipated initially *blush.*

As you *will see, the* crafting factor *is but* a small section of the over-all method *of* properly *pursuing contracts. But* considering that the talents *of* crafting *do* are inclined to *escape, and* given that *the* planning in the *tangible* doc is straight away gratifying, *we shall* focus *on this* element.

Planning *the* penned reaction *to an RFP (*Ask for *For Proposal)* is made up *of only* three techniques:

Examine *the customer's "Statement of Work" (SOW) and all accompanying "Instructions to Offerors".*
Put together an overview in the *proposal that* exactly *matches the* format laid out in *the SOW* and in *the* Directions *(*this is where *>98% of responders that* fail *the* grade, miss out on *the boat).*
Solution each individual issue on the ideal within your means *and* expertise. *Be concise and compact,* although not *obtuse.*
In looking through nevertheless *the* Guidance area you can be aware which the purchaser desires *the proposal* designed *in definite, separable sections. Your* reaction will have to, *I repeat,* ought to adhere to *these* Recommendations specifically.

Why?

The rationale for this assertion *goes* back *to how* Authorities organizations review *and* grade *proposals.*

Usually, *the smallest* Agency critique team which might be

assembled is made up of four *specialties:*

The program Supervisor in control of the general program. *He or his* workforce *is* liable for choosing *an Offeror's proposal* that may increase software accomplishment. He's *only* serious about *your* Administration *Summary. He* might or might not *be technically disposed.*
The Finance Supervisor *will* seem *at your proposal* from the *finance angle: is your* presenting financially acceptable*? Can a prudent* male *do the* operate required to the resources ideal*?*
The Plan Supervisor is barely enthusiastic about *your proposed* routine. Once again, *the "Prudent Man" rule is invoked: can the* get the job done *proposed be* accomplished while in the *time span* allocated*? Can* the different *subtasks spelled out* within the agenda *be* attained inside a well timed fashion*?*
The Specialized Supervisor is simply enthusiastic about *what* operate will be achieved. Will be the *proposed* alternative a reasonable tactic*? Is there any* noticeable parts of worry*? Are there implied traps,* for example *"And Then A* Wonder *Occurs". Does the offeror* comprehend the work being accomplished*? Does the offeror* understand *the* technical challenges from the career, and are *there undetected traps* for that *unwary?* Try to remember, in many conditions, *the* Technical Manager *understands the* technology particularly properly.
Put by yourself in their shoes *and* check with oneself *the* difficult issue*: "If I* were *the* Review *Board, would I give me a* contract*?* What is actually lacking *from this* response that will lead to *the* project *to* fall short*?"*

The other aspect that's generally ignored because of the *proposal initiate* is the client, in the majority of conditions, *will* intentionally *specify* the exact format which they choose to *see* during the *proposal.* Aspect *of that logic is* provided above during the *description* of the Review workforce. The greater refined aspect is always that the initial *sorting of proposals is* by the structure of the response. Should the structure with the response *matches the* said format within the Directions, *the proposal is* positioned within the *"Tentative" pile.*

Structure *does* make a difference.

In the event the structure would not *match the* Directions, *the proposal is* put while in the *"Hold" pile.* According to the quality on the *responses* within the *"Tentative" pile, any* supplying *that manages* to get into your *"Hold" pile* may *be discarded* with no studying. In case your *proposal* response finally ends up during the *"Hold" pile,* that you are nearly as good *as* eliminated correct within the get started, *and* your entire attempts *are for naught.*

CHAPTER 10

USING PREDICTIVE ANALYSIS TO BREAK THE CLUTTER

Predictive analytics is really a alternative utilized by several organizations right now to get extra price out of the large amounts of uncooked facts *by* applying tactics which have been utilized to predict upcoming *behaviors* inside of an organization, it is really purchaser foundation, it can be products and services. *Predictive analytics encompasses* various methods *from* facts *mining*, figures *and* game principle *that* analyze recent *and* historical facts to produce *predictions about* long run activities.

The advantages *of* implementing *predictive analytics is* simple. You will find many *documented* situation scientific studies *and* success stories the place *predictive* assessment *yielded* a considerable *return on* expenditure, served providers improve present procedures, presented an even better understanding *of* consumer habits, discovered unpredicted alternatives, *and* predicted challenges prior to *they* happened. *But with* each of the positive aspects associated *with predictive analytics*, there are plenty of problems *that accompany* becoming *an analytics-driven* business.

The perceived complexity would be the biggest problem dealing with *executives* these days. The fee *of implementation* is often a shut 2nd. Although these are typically legitimate *fears*, a lot of resources are now being formulated *to simplify* the process *and* set up *transparency* in the intricate formulation *and statically modeling*. It truly is, even so, as many as businesses to coach themselves on the essentials and ideas *of predictive* investigation in an effort to thoroughly employ *these* resources.

Yet another obstacle, that is extra technological, is definitely the conventional strategy of having *analyst* take a look at knowledge *sets by* conserving knowledge *and manually* applying interactions in order to *make predictive assumptions*. Even though this can operate at a basic stage *of predictive analytics, predictive analytics at* it can be only application needs really huge quantities of facts and thus *is* very best suited for *analytics platforms with parallel processing, which* aid tailor made *analytical* purposes that question info employing *SQL*.

This delivers *us* to a different challenge *with* implementing *predictive analytics* in the organization, and that *is* controlling the enormous knowledge *volumes* affiliated *with it. Some* organizations acknowledged to apply leading edge *analytical* methods, *are* accumulating *petabytes (*that's about one thousand *terabytes, or* 1 *million gigabytes)* of data. Though *these* quantities of knowledge have to have pricey info *warehouse* updates, *it* enables corporations *to* type extremely thorough *analytics and it* boosts *visitor/customer* practical experience *by* furnishing specific, custom made advertising and marketing *and* services.

But using these huge quantities of details *and* knowledge *storage* arrives *the* worries of manufacturing *the* system *for processing this* data *with* intricate formulas *at* rapid rates. As a result of *this, analytic platforms* generally run *off massively parallel processing (MPP) databases. MPP databases coordinate processing* of a single method *by* extra *than* just one *processor by dividing up* aspects of *a* method *into* numerous *processors with their* different *memory and* functioning techniques. *But* several companies that cannot pay for *MPP databases,* instead employ *analytical platforms as* info *marts to off-load* advanced *processing.*

Whilst *these* troubles *to* indeed appear for being intricate, *the* vital thing to understand is that should you possess the *architecture to* assist *it,* there are actually many tools to choose from *that* acquire *out the complexities and* applying *predictive modeling.*

CHAPTER 11

MORE ADVANCED PREDICTIVE ANALYSIS TECHNIQUES TO DERIVE INSIGHTS

Much more superior *predictive analytics* procedures consist of:

Time
Series
Forecasting
Details *Profiling and Transformations*
Bayesian Analytics Regression
Classification Dependency or Association Evaluation
Simulation Optimization

Time collection *forecasting predicts* the future value of *a* measure depending on past *values. Time* collection *forecasting* utilizes *a* model *to forecast* long term situations dependent on identified earlier activities. Examples incorporate inventory price ranges *and* product sales earnings.

Details *profiling and transformation* takes advantage of features *that* review *row and column* attributes *and dependencies,* improve facts *formats, merge fields,* mixture records, *and* sign up for *rows and columns.*

Bayesian analytics seize *the* ideas employed in chance *forecasting.* It is actually *a statistical* course of action *which estimate parameters* of the fundamental *distribution* depending on *the* noticed *distribution. An* instance *is* used in *a* courtroom placing *by* a person *juror to coherently accumulate the* proof *for and* in opposition to *the guilt* of your *defendant,* and also to *see* no matter if, *in totality, it* meets *their threshold for 'beyond* a reasonable *doubt'.*

Regression assessment is actually a *statistical* software for your *investigation of* associations in between *variables.* Generally, *the investigator seeks* to ascertain *the causal* impact of 1 *variable* on *another-the* impact of the cost enhance upon need, as an example, or perhaps the outcome *of* alterations while in the funds source upon *the inflation* rate.

Classification employed characteristics *in* information *to assign an* item to the *predefined* class *or* forecast the worth of the *numeric variable of* curiosity. Illustrations incorporate credit score chance assessment, likelihood to get. Illustrations consist of *acquisition, cross-sell, attrition,* credit *scoring and collections.*

Clustering or segmentation separates knowledge *into homogeneous subgroups* based on attributes. *Clustering assigns a* established *of observations into subsets (clusters)* in order that *observations* in the same *cluster are* equivalent. *An* illustration *is* consumer *demographic segmentation.*

Dependency or association analysis *describes* sizeable *associations* amongst details objects. *An* case in point *is* marketplace *basket* analysis. Market place *basket* examination is a *modeling* procedure primarily based upon the speculation *that* if you buy a specific group of items, you will be far more *(or* less*)* probably to purchase one more team of things.

Simulation styles *a* method construction *to estimate the* effect *of* management decisions *or* improvements. *Simulation* design habits *will* transform *in* every *simulation* in accordance with *the* set *of* preliminary *parameters assumed* for that setting. Illustrations contain stock *reorder* guidelines, forex *hedging,* military services training.

Optimization versions *a* method structure when it comes to *constraints* to discover the very best answer. *Optimization* types form part of the greater method which people *use* to help you *them make* choices. *The* user is ready to influence *the* answers *which the* model provides *and* assessments *them* before creating *a* remaining selection regarding how to proceed. Illustrations contain *scheduling of* shift personnel, *routing of* teach *cargo, and pricing airline seats.*

CHAPTER 12

LAUNCHING PAID SURVEYS TO REDUCE COST AND GET QUICK RESULTS. WORKING WITH MODERN ONLINE PANEL PARTNER OR COMPANIES IN MARKET RESEARCH WORLD AS AN AGENCY OR FREELANCER MR CONSULTANT

Paid current market investigate is a wonderful *way for* organizations to learn about their *customer's likes and* choices. Moreover compensated current market investigate is an *earning* prospect with the *entrepreneurial minded* who would like to get paid *to share their* thoughts. Information and facts *gleaned from* people as a result of current market study is undoubtedly an priceless software. *This* wealth of data is often *instrumental* from the progress *of* products and services *from* begin to complete.

Compensated sector exploration *can* are available distinctive kinds. For illustration *some* market researchers *use* emphasis groups. Concentration groups may well *get* collectively *in* man or woman *or* on the net. *These* groups *are* meant to reflect the diversity *inherent* from the basic public. Also, *a participant in* marketplace research may perhaps *partake* in an interview *(*on the internet *or off)* where *their* views *and* opinions *are* carefully *examined. Also* paid out industry research may possibly are available in the form *of* on the net *surveys. These* on the net *surveys* are getting to be progressively well known, given that they *are* easy to the *participant* as well as the market exploration firm.

One more *way* market investigation *is* made use of *is by* acquiring shoppers compose product or service reviews. Current market *surveys* attempt to generate appropriate questions inside a reasonable *way* that is agent with the bigger population. *When* used successfully, paid out current market exploration *can* produce applicable information about how *a* supplied products will probably be gained and how to improve income.

By assessing *the* beliefs *and* preferences directly from the consumer, a firm *can* build products which attract *their* clientele *in* each *way*. One example is, little distinctions inside the design and style of the item could make *or* split *the* item when it comes to marketing and advertising achievements. Moreover, enter *from* consumers supplied directly by paid current market investigation, *can* expose *what packaging and* advertising truly *sells the* products. For this reason intelligent companies *are* paying out very good funds for your personal insight *and* views. They're ready to accomplish that since there's no far better approach to know what customers are searching for *than* heading directly to *the* source.

Additionally, paid promoting pros *are* skilled *to interpret* the data *these surveys* make *in* helpful *and insightful* methods. The information received *from these surveys* can be made use of *to* project *what* buyers *will want* from the upcoming. The result is product progress *and* promoting becomes *a dynamic* procedure that is still new and leading edge. Thanks for the efforts *of* paid survey *takers,* marketing has not *been so* enjoyable.

Market research utilizing *surveys is* quickly, uncomplicated *and* gives knowledge *at* an amazing pace. Information and facts is usually *recorded and analyzed in* 50 percent time *it took* applying old fashion methods of *surveys.* People that *are* paid *to* be involved in *this* investigation benefit ideal absent *in two* approaches, initially they have the moment *gratification of* understanding *their* belief *is valued and* next given that they get paid excellent funds to precise those self same viewpoints.

Participation in paid industry investigation is simple and easy also. *Most surveys* get *mere minutes* to finish. *Some surveys are* extended, even so the payment helps make the time and energy value *it.* In addition, *the* solutions *and surveys in* concern *are* daily items that they may be probably quite knowledgeable about. There aren't any unique competencies *or* training *to* bear, just *a* honest *willingness* to express *your* thoughts by using a *well-defined and* detailed survey. Many of *these surveys are taken* on-line, and are *as* handy *as clicking a mouse.* The point that *the* study *is* performed on-line helps make *it* reliable, much too. There is certainly *no* area *for* creative *interpretation* within your answers *like there* could possibly be which has a study carried out in the standard style. On the net paid out *surveys* can offer businesses *with* individuals instantaneous answers that could enable them to maintain *their edge* over the global industry. In addition, they might count on accuracy down to *a mere* portion *of* error.

Paid out market place investigation may include remaining *invited to* participate in a spotlight group. Having said that, for several people these kinds of *face-to-face* situations aren't functional *or* fascinating. For those who want to indicator nearly participate in market place investigation, but not depart *the* consolation in their property online *surveys are* abundant.

Privacy is often a concern *for* current market investigate members. Businesses *that* employ individuals *to* get on the net *surveys,* typically thoroughly defend personalized info in the contributors. *This assures* shoppers they will not *be swamped with spammers* whenever they *consent to* choose one particular on the net survey *or* whenever they participate in twenty.

As a way to be described as a *panelist for* online *surveys and* compensated market analysis, *the participant* should *be invited.* Mainly because *these* marketing applications *are scientifically engineered* to get consultant from the broader industry, *eligibility* in a very survey *or* focus group could *be* depending on assembly particular *demographics* that the organization is looking for. Any time a *panelist is* decided on *for participation,* they are going to be *invited to* take part. *Some* compensated industry investigate *panelists are compensated by a* set charge. Many others *are entered into drawings, and* even now other people *will* obtain absolutely free *or discounted* products as an *incentive* to join.

Entrepreneurial people who find themselves motivated *to* get paid cash carrying out market investigation indicator *up with* companies *as* likely members. You can find *an* ample opportunity to *make* very good dollars *in* industry research *by* collaborating within a number of current market analysis routines, which include on the web *surveys,* product or service evaluations *and* emphasis teams. Market place exploration organizations *will* carry out *an* job interview *with* likely *respondents,* to get a distinct *demographic profile.* It is essential to take note listed here *that these* companies *are* typically pretty *conscientious about* shielding individual info. It is actually in reality *an* field normal *for* current market analysis to do *so.* Immediately after *signing up* that has a paid market place analysis corporation, people *are* normally totally free to sign up for less than *the* assignments they would like to. *Some* may well elect to *only* take part in online *surveys,* while some will discover concentrate teams additional for their *liking.* In any case, this may *be* a fascinating, exciting way to *make* further earnings. For some this might *be* an excellent job that has positive aspects this kind of *as* adaptability, doing work days *and* several hours of their choosing, and also the capability to create income *at their leisure. This* compensated marketplace investigate is usually a profitable problem for everybody associated, delivering *in-depth* facts *for* businesses *and* with the customer may also profit *by* owning *their* opinions depend *and by supplementing their incomes.*

CHAPTER 13

MARKET RESEARCH FOR DIGITAL OR ECOMMERCE BUSINESSES

After you *practice in research* Web, you probably have already got a certain target marketplace in your mind. You already know the sort of individuals *comprising this* market place, and you simply also have a transparent notion of *the* companies which they may possibly obtain beneficial *and* helpful. Needless to say, *your* systems, services *are all directed* to supply responses *or* options to their desires. *If* anything *goes* well, you may manage to sell *your* products and services routinely to the rising market. Alternatively, *how will you* take care of your situation in case your precise gross sales effectiveness *is way off your* gross sales focus on?

Here is the prevalent problem confronted *by* lots of on the internet services suppliers. Should you end up in the middle of a similar predicament *then* it's a must that you simply identify the foundation cause of the dilemma. This situation is frequently because of *a disparity* amongst whatever you *are* furnishing *and what your* goal marketplace seriously wishes. You could possibly *only be* providing *them* companies depending on *your assumptions* instead of automatically depending on the actual wants and needs of the target market.

It is possible to *extricate* on your own *from this* restricted resolve or simply stay clear of this example by just executing industry research. Current market investigate must *be* included within your *menu of specialties* if you need to grasp just what *are your* focus on *market's* fears *and* pursuits. You have to understand *the* matters that they are having difficulties *with and* for that reason *formulate* ways in an effort to tackle *them.* You must give *them* alternatives to their challenges. *No* degree of optimistic *reinforcement* to produce a favorable *imaging* will make *them* invest in *your* products or services in case you will not be capable *to* influence *them* you are supplying answers for their complications.

It is also crucial that you observe market place study in the common basis. This really is for the reason that *new* issues *and* fears may perhaps crop up each from time to time, and you also need to be *vigilant* and prepared to respond to these problems in order for yourself to not retain *your* connection with your clients *and* safeguard *your* market place *share.*

Current market investigation does not have for being *a million-dollar* task. It truly is not really important for yourself to face on the street *and distribute flyers or* study *sheets.* One of essentially the most practical approaches *of conducting* current market exploration will be to involve a brief study with your *sign-up* web site. Check with engaging issues about their largest problem from the particular specialized niche that you're concentrating on. As a result, it's possible you'll *pose a follow-up* query by having an *auto-responder* for the *most* probable solutions. *Conducting an* annual or simply a *semi-annual* survey will likely assist you hold track with the worries *and* issues of *your* marketplace *and* anticipate adjustments in their buying preferences *and* pursuits.

CHAPTER 14

WINNING OVER INSIGHTFUL REPORTS PERSUADING CLIENTS

There is just one crucial distinction between experiences and many *other* forms *of* small business producing, *and we* obtain a hint *of that* while in the word, *"report."* Whereas *with* numerous *other* types *of* composed *comes* you could become a very little innovative *and* set your individual *slant* on the phrases, inside of a *report* it's essential to *not. Not in* principle, anyway.

Within a *report,* you're supposed *to report - not embellish, embroider,* affect, etc. *Just the* specifics *and* nothing at all nevertheless the details.

This doesn't, even so, suggest *that* reports have to have for being uninteresting *and* dull. *It does,* however, imply you cannot *make the* information additional exciting *than* it really is. Impossible? *No, it just* will take *some* good firm *and* very clear crafting.

Ahead of *we go any* more, there are many books *and* coaching programs on the market *that* train *you the formalities and practicalities of report* crafting. *Some* tend to be more *long-winded than* others. A lot of *them are* superior.

Right here in the following paragraphs I am unable to *do what other writers do* within a book, therefore if you might want to publish experiences quite a bit, I like to recommend which you acquire a single *or two* of your most popular publications *and* analyze *them. What* I am doing in this article *then,* should be to highlight *the* details I think *are* most critical to help you *make your* reports additional *readable,* plus the info *in them* appear throughout far more *vividly.*

For those who perform in a very much larger business, there will probably *be* set *formats for* stories, at least for your interior wide range. No matter if you like *them or not* you are generally *obliged* to stay *to them.* Nevertheless just how *you roll out and* write *your* content material continues to be nearly *you.*

So what are classified as the critical details *to* concentration *on?*

1. Compose for the *reader*

Will not make it possible for by yourself *to* drop *into "business" jargon and phrasing* irrespective of the amount of *you or* others could experience it can be much more suitable. It is not. *Use language and tone of voice* that your crucial visitors *will* experience cozy *with.* If you don't understand what *they* really feel at ease *with,* uncover *out.* It truly is well truly worth getting the difficulty, due to the fact it'll *make the report* significantly far more satisfying *for them to* study - a great *reflection on you.*

If your *report* would be to *be* read through *by* numerous types of different *audiences,* target *your language* over the primary groups. Ensure that less *topic-literate* visitors *are catered for* by making use of *discreet explanations of* technical phrases or maybe a short *glossary of* conditions as an *appendix* throughout the *report.*

2. Organize *your* information and facts *sensibly*

Commence *by* composing yourself *out* an inventory

of headings which start out for the starting *and* complete together with the *conclusions* of one's information. In the event you should consist of a good deal *of* background information before you go into *the "meat"* in the data, section *it off* obviously *with headings that* mention that it really is background *("Research* Venture Objectives," *"Research* Approaches Utilised *To Collate* Info," *"Personnel* Concerned *In Questionnaire,"* etcetera.) *so* those that realize it *all* presently *can skip straight* into the crucial stuff.

Make certain *your headings "tell the story" so* another person *glancing* via individuals on your own can get the essential *messages.* (You will see that fast paced *executives will* thanks *for* doing *this,* specially when they *have* sixteen *other,* equivalent reviews *to* read within a *crowded commuter* prepare within the *way* right into a assembly to discuss *all* of them.) *Then fill* during the facts below each *heading as concisely* as you *can.*

3. *Use an "executive summary"* to tell *it* in the *nutshell*

Depending about the mother nature of one's *report* you could possibly *be* expected to include *an* government *summary, or* at least *an introduction that captures* the main element points of your respective data. The target of this would be to provide the *reader* the real key problems *as* speedily as feasible. Generate *this* soon after you've done your body in the *report, not* right before. Make use of your list *of headings* being a information.

Retain *strictly* for the specifics - this can be still part of *the report, not your interpretation of it. Strip* every single *sentence* all the way down to *bare bones with* minimum *adjectives and adverbs. Use* shorter phrases *and sentences.* You should not *just* get to the purpose - start off *with it and* stick with *it.*

4. If your *interpretation* is known as *for,* keep *it* different

If section of *your remit* will be to comment on *the report and/or its conclusions,* continue to keep *this* independent in the primary overall body of information. *(Blocked off* inside of a *box or* less than *a* evidently divided *heading will do.)*

The natural way *as* you're expert you're going to be *as* objective as is possible. But if you do really feel *strongly* one *way or* yet another, be sure that *your argument is* put *as* fairly as feasible with out heading *on for* webpages *and* internet pages. Don't forget, temporary is beautiful, while it really is more difficult to put in writing *briefly (and* involve each of the important points*) than* it is actually to supply text *in abundance.*

5. Really don't *get carried* away *with illustrations*

Graphs and charts are perfect as an instance vital troubles *and* similar to the gentleman mentioned, *"a* photo *is* worthy of *a thousand* phrases.*"* Nevertheless be sure that individuals you employ *are* of the amount of *complexity* that should *be* comprehended because of the very least *topic-literate* of the audience. There is nothing at all additional annoying than a *graph that* usually takes *you* 20 *minutes to decipher.* It's *not* a great deal of *a* scenario *that* audience *are* way too stupid to be aware of a fancy *graph,* because it is usually that they don't would like to spend far too a lot *time* functioning *it out. The easier/quicker you* make it *for* readers to grasp *and assimilate your* facts, the more profitable *your report.*

Consider, *also,* to maintain *graphs and charts* bodily *adjacent* into the text *that talks* regarding the identical detail. You can find nothing at all far more annoying for that *reader* when they really need to keep *flipping from* entrance *to* back again of the document. *(When* unsure, consider of someone reading *your report on that crowded commuter* prepare.*)*

6. Cut *the* clutter

However *on that* subject matter, consider to avoid which include a lot of various things as part of your *report,* despite how long *and* concerned it is. Should you *do* need to incorporate *appendices and* various *bits of* track record material, investigate studies, etc., make certain they're *neatly labeled and contained* within the back again within your doc.

As I recommended before, never talk to visitors *to skip* backwards and forwards, *directing them with asterisks* and other *reference directing symbols.* When you are producing *a* health-related *report or paper then* you might be *obliged* to include *these when quoting references from other papers, but* please retain *even these* to some minimum. They're really *distracting* and will break *your reader's* concentration.

7. Choose *some* hassle to make *it* look good

I am aware you should not decide *a* guide *by its* go over, *but* persons *do. Like it or not.* In accordance with United kingdom Graphic consultant *Tessa S,* when you walk right into a meeting, *55%* of your initial perception of somebody *is* mirrored completely during the *way* you might be *dressed.* Documents tumble to the identical gap. *So how your* document appears to be like *goes* a lengthy approach to building the proper impression of the perform, *and of you.*

Obviously *if a report* is due to *go* outdoors *your* firm *and* specially *to* clientele *or* consumers, you will be cautious to make sure it really is *polished and* evidently *branded* along with your corporate identity *and* all that. Nevertheless, *how an* inner *report* appears is crucial, also, while *your Head of Finance* might need *apoplexy* if you *bind it in* expensive shiny *card. Be* practical while using the inside selection - *neat, understated, groomed* appears to be like never really have to value much nevertheless they *"say"* a great deal regarding the value of your respective *report (*and you also.*)*

8. *A* moment *on minutes*

I think *minute-taking* is a terrible job, possessing performed *so* for 6 several years though with a *charity fundraising committee. And* currently being worthless *at handwriting (*thanks *to* decades *of* computer systems *and typewriters)* by no means intellect *shorthand (was thrown* away from *secretarial* college right after three weeks*) I struggled* *for months to scribble* all the things down to selling price later, right up until I realized *that my* mind *was* a far more productive *filter* of knowledge.

At the end of every *agenda* merchandise, *I* asked *myself the* basic *reporter* thoughts *of "who, what,* exactly where, *when, why, how* and how significantly.*" All* I'd to carry out *was jot down* a number of phrases *and* once i bought house *to my trusty* Computer system, *I could* expand these *into* realistic *summaries of what went on.* Just as much on the *dialogue in* conferences *is* possibly unnecessary, *repetitive, or* the two, merely use your brain as a *filter.* Which is *what* it can be skilled to complete to suit your needs in the *day-to-day* lifetime, *so* it works *for* conferences too.

A single word *of warning* nevertheless*;* never wait around also extensive prior to *your* function *up your minutes.* Yet another *trick the* brain *does* will be to ignore soon after several hours or maybe a working day *or so at most...*

ABOUT THE AUTHOR

'Farid Premani takes us through a myriad of information on how and why new age companies should use data science predictive analysis. Each page beholds a well of information that helps market research companies benefit in their project endeavors in more ways than one innovatively using modern research tools and analysis through big data'

'Farid Premani, as an expert consultant on market research, uses this book as an outlet to share all his expertise and professionalism to create this bible for agencies and independent research consultants. He has given us a detailed flow of structure to make it easier for even the common businesses and startup agencies to learn and implement expertise of data research and understanding what customer wants in 2016'

www.ingramcontent.com/pod-product-compliance
Lightning Source LLC
Chambersburg PA
CBHW060416190526
45169CB00002B/920
* 9 7 8 1 5 3 7 0 8 2 4 6 2 *